I am worthy of love
and respect.

I am capable of

achieving my goals.

I choose to let go of
fear and embrace
love.

I trust in my
abilities to overcome
challenges.

I am grateful for
all the blessings in
my life.

I am surrounded by positivity and abundance.

I am confident in
my decisions and
choices.

I am deserving of
happiness and
fulfillment.

I am in control of my thoughts and emotions.

I am constantly growing and improving.

I am at peace with
myself and the
world around me.

I am open to new
opportunities and
experiences.

I am strong and
resilient in the
face of adversity.

I am enough just as
I am.

I am capable of creating a life I love.

I am grateful for my unique talents and abilities.

I am worthy of

success and

prosperity.

I am surrounded by loving and supportive people.

I am capable of making a positive difference in the world.

I trust in the universe to guide me towards my highest good.

I am deserving of
love and happiness.

I am abundant in
all areas of my life.

I am grateful for
the lessons I have
learned in life.

I am confident in
my ability to
overcome any
obstacle.

I am open to
receiving all the
good the universe
has to offer.

I am constantly learning and growing.

I am worthy of
respect and
admiration.

I am capable of
achieving anything
I set my mind to.

I am grateful for
my health and
wellbeing.

I am at peace with my past and excited for my future.

I am surrounded by positivity and good energy.

I am confident in
my ability to make
the right decisions.

I am deserving of
all the good things
in life.

I am strong,
capable and
resilient.

I am grateful for
the love and
support of my
friends and
family.

I am open to

receiving all the

abundance the

universe has to

offer.

I am capable of creating a life that brings me joy and fulfillment.

I am worthy of

success and

prosperity in all

areas of my life.

I am confident in
my ability to
manifest my
dreams and desires.

I am surrounded by
people who uplift
and inspire me.

I am grateful for
the opportunities
that come my way.

I am deserving of
love, respect and
happiness.

I am capable of overcoming any obstacle in my path.

I am open to new

experiences and

opportunities.

I am constantly
growing and
evolving.

I am worthy of the
life I desire.

I am confident in
my abilities to
achieve my goals.

I am grateful for
all the lessons life
has taught me.

I am at peace with myself and the world around me.

I am surrounded by
love and positivity.

I am capable of

creating a life that

is meaningful and

fulfilling.

I am deserving of
all the good things
that come into my
life.

I am strong and
resilient in the
face of challenges.

I am grateful for
the abundance in
my life.

I am confident in

my ability to make

the right choices

for myself.

I am worthy of love, respect and admiration.

I am open to receiving all the good things the universe has to offer.

I am capable of
achieving anything
I set my mind to.

I am surrounded by people who believe in me.

I am grateful for
all the blessings in
my life.

I am deserving of happiness and fulfillment.

I am confident in my ability to overcome any obstacle.

I am at peace with myself and the world around me.

I am capable of creating a life I love.

I am worthy of

success and

prosperity.

I am surrounded by

positivity and good

energy.

I am grateful for

the opportunities

that come my way.

I am confident in
my ability to
achieve my dreams.

I am deserving of love, respect and happiness.

I am capable of

making a positive

difference in the

world.

I am open to

receiving all the

abundance the

universe has to

offer.

I am strong and resilient in the face of challenges.

I am grateful for
all the lessons life
has taught me.

I am confident in my ability to make the right decisions.

I am deserving of

all the good things

in life.

I am capable of creating a life that brings me joy and fulfillment.

I am worthy of
success and
prosperity in all
areas of my life.

I am surrounded by
people who uplift
and inspire me.

I am grateful for
all the love and
support in my life.

I am confident in my ability to overcome any obstacle.

I am deserving of happiness and fulfillment.

I am open to new

experiences and

opportunities.

I am capable of
achieving anything
I set my mind to.

I am grateful for
the abundance in
my life.

I am confident in
my ability to
manifest my
dreams and desires.

I am worthy of
love, respect and
admiration.

I am surrounded by positivity and good energy.

I am capable of
creating a life that
is meaningful and
fulfilling.

I am deserving of
all the good things
that come into my
life.

I am strong and
resilient in the
face of challenges.

I am grateful for
the opportunities
that come my way.

I am confident in
my ability to make
the right choices
for myself.

I am deserving of
all the love and
happiness in the
world.

I am open to

receiving all the

abundance the

universe has to

offer.

I am capable of
achieving anything
I set my mind to.

I am surrounded by people who support and uplift me.

I am grateful for
all the blessings in
my life.

I am confident in
my ability to
overcome any
obstacle.

I am worthy of success and prosperity.

I am capable of creating a life I love and deserve.